SECRET OF THE PUKING PENGUINS

...AND MORE!

BY ANA MARÍA RODRÍGUEZ

ANIMAL SECRETS REVEALED!

Enslow Publishers, Inc.
40 Industrial Road
Box 398
Berkeley Heights, NJ 07922
USA

http://www.enslow.com

Acknowledgments

The author would like to express her immense gratitude to all the scientists who have contributed to the *Animal Secrets Revealed!* series. Their comments and photos have been invaluable to the creation of these books.

Library of Congress Cataloging-in-Publication Data

Rodriguez, Ana Maria, 1958–
  Secret of the puking penguins— and more! / Ana María Rodríguez.
      p. cm.
  Summary: "Explains how King penguin fathers preserve food in their stomachs for their chicks and details other strange abilities of different types of animals"—Provided by publisher.
  Includes bibliographical references and index.
  ISBN-13: 978-0-7660-2955-2
  ISBN-10: 0-7660-2955-7
  1. Reptiles—Juvenile literature. 2. Reptiles—Research—Juvenile literature. 3. Birds—Juvenile literature. 4. Birds—Research—Juvenile literature. I. Title.
  QL644.2.R636 2009
  597.9—dc22   2007039490

Printed in the United States of America

10 9 8 7 6 5 4 3 2 1

To Our Readers: We have done our best to make sure all Internet Addresses in this book were active and appropriate when we went to press. However, the author and the publisher have no control over and assume no liability for the material available on those Internet sites or on other Web sites they may link to. Any comments or suggestions can be sent by e-mail to comments@enslow.com or to the address on the back cover.

♻ Enslow Publishers, Inc., is committed to printing our books on recycled paper. The paper in every book contains 10% to 30% post-consumer waste (PCW). The cover board on the outside of each book contains 100% PCW. Our goal is to do our part to help young people and the environment too!

Illustration Credits: Dr. Adam Britton, Crocodilian.com, Australia, pp. 18, 19; Dr. Daphne Soares, University of Maryland, p. 16; Dr. Jay Meyers, Northern Arizona University, p. 9; Dr. Nick Davies, Cambridge University, pp. 29, 30, 32, 33; Frans Lanting/Minden Pictures, p. 23; Jupiterimages Corporation/Photos.com, pp. 7, 21, 25, 37, 38; New York Times, Proceedings of the National Academy of Sciences and Fudan University, p. 40.

Cover Illustration: Jupiterimages Corporation/Photos.com.

★ CONTENTS ★

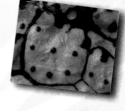

ENTER THE WORLD OF ANIMAL SECRETS!

n this volume of *Animal Secrets Revealed!*, you will discover what amazing things reptiles and birds can do. Accompany American scientists as they observe chameleons very closely and reveal the secret of the chameleon's powerful tongue. Join another American scientist as she uncovers one of the secrets that make alligators one of the oldest hunters on Earth. Travel with French scientists to one of the coldest places on the planet and find out how king penguin parents manage to pre- serve food in their bodies to feed their newborn baby chicks. Then join British scientists as they learn why cuckoo birds might be considered "masters of disguise." Finally, travel to China and find out how the peacock gets its magnificent colors. Welcome to the world of animal secrets!

1
WHAT A GRIP!

Scientist Anthony Herrel has always been fascinated by chameleons. However, he says, "My real interest started after I watched one of them catch another lizard. That was truly spectacular and immediately sparked my curiosity on how they can do this."[1]

Sticky and Rough Is Not Enough

Two things give the chameleon's tongue some of its super grip. One is sticky mucus, a goo that covers the tongue. The second is a rough surface. The chameleon's tongue has a lot of tiny bumps, ridges, and pits on its surface. A bumpy tongue covered in sticky mucus seems enough to easily grab crickets and flies, which are the favorite foods of small chameleons.[2]

5

Catching large prey, however, is another story. Large chameleons can grow to be as big as small cats and they can eat birds and lizards that weigh as much as 15 percent of the chameleon's weight.[3]

Herrel decided to uncover the secret of the chameleon's super tongue. He worked with Jay Meyers and together they closely watched chameleons eat. The chameleon's tongue is so fast, however, that they could not see how the tongue worked. They decided to take a closer— and slower—look at the chameleon's tongue in action.

Slooww Moootion . . .

To slow down the action, Herrel and Meyers used high speed video to record how chameleons feed. Then they watched the videos in slow motion.

The scientists placed a chameleon on a branch (one of their best performers was Precious, a beautiful female of the species *Furcifer oustaleti*).[4] Then they placed a cricket on a stick for Precious to eat. They turned the camera on and waited. After filming many chameleons and watching the movies in slow motion, Herrel and Meyers discovered something nobody had seen before.

There are different types of chameleons that vary in size, color, and shape. However, they all have long, sticky tongues with the power of suction to capture prey.

Discovering the Tongue's Secret

When the scientists watched the movie slowly, frame by frame, they discovered that just before the tongue touches the prey, muscles on each side of the tongue pull inward on the tip. This pulling forms a small bag or pouch on the tip that works like a suction cup. Mucus and the tongue's rough surface hold the prey while the pouch surrounds it. Finally, the tongue yanks the prey right into the mouth.[5]

> **Science Tongue Twister:**
> *Herrel and Meyers studied chameleons of various sizes. The smallest chameleon was* **Rhampholeon spectrum** *and the largest* **Chameleo melleri.**

Two strong muscles give the tongue its speed and power. One of the muscles shoots the tongue out of the chameleon's mouth with lightning speed. When the other muscle contracts, it pulls the tongue back into the mouth.[6] Scientists call the second muscle a "supermuscle" because it can shorten much more than a normal muscle.[7]

The scientists calculated that about 70 percent of all the tongue's power comes from the suction-cup effect. The rest of the grip power comes from the sticky mucus and the rough surface.[8] After studying many different types of chameleons, Herrel and Meyers realized that not only large chameleons but all chameleons have the power of suction in their tongues. "It just looks much more impressive when the

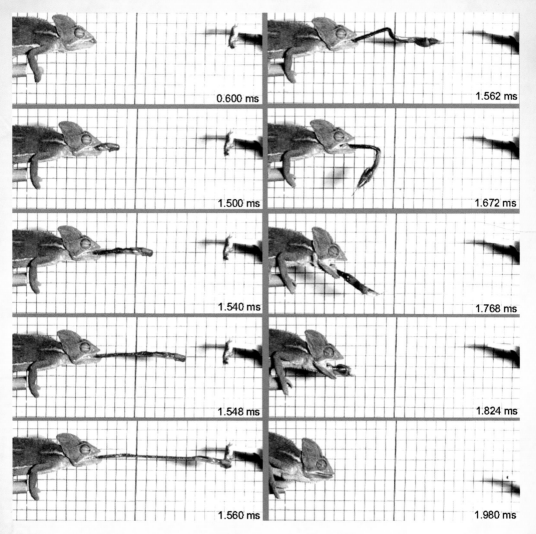

0.600 ms

1.562 ms

1.500 ms

1.672 ms

1.540 ms

1.768 ms

1.548 ms

1.824 ms

1.560 ms

1.980 ms

This sequence of photos taken by Dr. Jay Meyers shows how a veiled chameleon (*Chamaeleo calyptratus*) projects its tongue to capture a cricket. All ten frames of action happen in less than a second!

LONG TONGUE

Chameleons' size ranges from about three to forty-five centimeters long (1.2 to 18 inches). A chameleon's tongue can be as long as about one and a half times its body length, not including the tail! How does it cram such a long tongue inside its mouth? They coil it in a complex, packed way.[11]

big guys do it because they catch things like birds and lizards," instead of little crickets, said Herrel.[9]

Herrel and Meyers wondered why the suction power is useful to the chameleon. Herrel explains, "The suction power lets the animals capture much larger prey than would be possible using sticky forces alone. When you are sitting still on a branch, this may be the only meal you get in a while. A powerful tongue helps make sure that you can grab that meal!"[10]

The scientists have uncovered the secret of the chameleon tongue's powerful grip. Special muscles shape the tongue's tip like a suction cup that gets a tight grip on prey. Then supermuscles pull the prey into their mouths. The power of suction allows chameleons to fill their empty stomachs with one big meal instead of having to hunt for many small meals to satisfy their appetites.

Test the Power of Suction

In this experiment you will compare the grabbing power of goo to the power of suction using balloons, goo, and a suction cup.

Materials
★ 2 small balloons, deflated ★ paper
★ 1 small suction cup ★ Styrofoam
★ goo (see recipe below) ★ cardboard
★ tile wall, a single tile, or another surface the suction cup will attach to (smooth, non-porous, and clean)

Procedure
1. Cut one piece each of paper, Styrofoam, and cardboard in the following sizes:

paper	1 cm x 1 cm	5 cm x 5 cm
Styrofoam (use a cup)	1 cm x 1 cm	5 cm x 5 cm
cardboard	1 cm x 1 cm	5 cm x 5 cm

2. Line up the pieces on top of a paper-covered surface. Cover the tip of the empty balloon with goo.
3. Touch the goo-covered balloon to the cut-out pieces one by one and try to lift them. Which pieces did the gooey balloon lift? Which did it not?
4. Try to stick the gooey balloon to the tile wall. Does it stick? For how long?

BUILT FOR SPEED

We now know the suction-cup effect of the chameleon's tongue tip provides a strong grip. But what provides the extreme speed of the tongue? Scientists Jurriaan de Groot and Johan van Leeuwen from Holland discovered that when a chameleon shoots its tongue, the tip of the tongue accelerates, or speeds up, to five times the acceleration of a fighter jet! The tongue achieves this magnificent speed thanks to a unique catapult mechanism. The power for this mechanism comes from an elastic part of the tongue that resembles a "sliding spring."[12] It looks like a spring whose rings pack themselves like the tubes of a telescope, instead of stacking on each other like a slinky. When the sliding spring releases its force, the tip of the tongue accelerates faster than a jet and captures lunch much faster than the blink of an eye![13]

5. Compare the results with the balloon to the suction cup. Stick the suction cup to the tile. How long does it stay on the tile?
6. Using a hook piercing the open end of the balloon, hang different things from the balloon until it falls from the wall. For example, hang scissors, pens, or other small supplies.

Goo Recipe

Materials
★ Styrofoam cup
★ water
★ cornstarch
★ spoon
★ food coloring

Procedure
1. Measure five teaspoons of water into the cup. Add four drops of food coloring.
2. Add one quarter cup of cornstarch and mix slowly with the spoon, making sure there are no lumps. Set the cup aside for about one minute.
3. The goo should flow like a liquid but feel thicker—like slime—when touched with the fingers. Add one pinch of cornstarch at a time if the goo is too runny. Add a quarter teaspoon of water at a time if it is too thick to flow. Keep it covered to avoid further drying.
4. Do not dispose of the goo in the sink. It will clog the drain.

2
ALLIGATOR FEELINGS

Daphne Soares was sitting on the back of a huge bull alligator. Luckily, the ferocious reptile was well tied up! She and her colleagues were cruising along a steaming hot Louisiana swamp in a pick-up truck transporting the alligator from one area to another.

Soares looked at the alligator's jaw. She saw many, probably a thousand black spots on the animal's face. They looked like a beard that was beginning to grow and they felt bumpy too. She wondered, "What are those little spots for?"[1]

Baby Gator's Surprise

Working with fully grown alligators was definitely out of the question. Soares says, "Alligators are made for closing their jaws. An adult can close its mouth with thousands of pounds of pressure per square inch."[2] This is enough to crush even the hardest bones.

Actually, alligators come out of their eggs biting, but then their bites are not very dangerous. Soares knows this firsthand. One day she was watching a baby alligator hatching when she was bitten. She tells the story, "I tried to help him and peel off the shell

> **Meet the Scientists:**
> *Daphne Soares is a neuroscientist (a scientist who studies the nervous system) interested in understanding how birds and alligators hear and communicate through sound.*

when he suddenly bit my finger! I gave out a humiliating eeek! He was clamped on pretty good so I had to walk around the lab for at least five minutes attached to this ferocious little life. It didn't hurt at all so I didn't want to yank him. I just waited for him to give up. But boy, was I surprised when it happened!"[3]

Baby alligators are not a big threat, but by the time they are two years old (and about sixty centimeters long), they become very aggressive and chomp ferociously. So Soares decided to study the secret of the black spots in very young alligators only up to two years old. Baby alligators have the spots and are easier and safer to handle than bigger ones. She gathered about thirty young alligators and cared for them in hot-tub-like pools at the Woods Hole Oceanographic Institute in Massachusetts.

Testing the Sensors

Soares had the idea that the bumpy spots were sensors, so she set up a series of experiments to determine what type of sensors they were. She decided to test different stimuli, or things like light, electrical currents, and even stinky things, one at a time to see which one activated the sensors.

When animal sensors are activated, the nerves that connect them to the brain produce tiny electrical signals that carries the message to the brain. For instance, when you taste a piece of chocolate, your taste sensors—taste buds—in your tongue fire electrical signals through nerves that reach the brain. You know then how sweet chocolate is.

By measuring the electrical activity in the nerves coming from the spots, Soares would know if a stimulus, light for example, was detected by the spots. If there was electrical activity when light hit the sensors,

Dr. Daphne Soares holds a small American alligator she captured in the wild. Notice how she keeps the alligator's mouth closed with her hand to avoid a surprise bite.

then the spots would be light sensors. If there was no electrical activity when light hit the sensors, then most likely the spots would not be light sensors.

Soares prepared her baby alligators so she could measure electrical signals in the nerves coming from the spots. For this, she first anesthetized the alligators, putting them temporarily to sleep. Then, she connected special tiny electrodes to the nerves. This does not hurt the baby gators. The electrodes were connected to a computer that would display nerve activity, if there was any.[4]

Soares placed the alligator carrying the electrodes in a water

> **Science Tongue Twister:**
> *Scientists call the alligators that Soares studied* Alligator mississippiensis, *also called* American alligator.

tank and provided one stimulus, light, to the alligator. She watched the computer to see if the stimulus activated the sensors, but light did not activate them. Neither did electrical currents nor stinky scents.[5] What could the stimulus be?

A Lucky Accident Uncovers the Secret

Soares was wondering what other stimuli to test when she experienced a lucky mishap. She explains, "I had dropped something in the tank and as I reached for it, I created surface waves—ripples in the water—with my hand."[6] At this moment, the electrodes registered that the nerves from the alligator's

Alligators and crocodiles both have spots on their faces that sense ripples in the water. This photo of the head of a saltwater crocodile (*Crocodylus porosus*) shows the pressure sensors clearly.

spots had fired a signal. The sensors were sensitive to ripples in the water!

Chomp, Chomp, Chomp!

Next, Soares wanted to know if the alligators had any use for these pressure sensors. She placed a young alligator in the water tank. She blocked the animal's ears with petroleum jelly so it could not hear and turned off the lights so it could not see. Then, she dropped a single drop of water in the tank.[7]

Using infrared light to see what was going on in the tank, Soares saw that even though the alligator could not hear or see, when one drop of water fell in the tank, the animal bit at it! When Soares covered the spots on the alligator's face so it could not feel the ripples, the animal did not respond at all. Only when the spot sensors were uncovered did the alligator respond to the falling drops of water by turning and snapping full force![8]

Soares had discovered the secret of the sensitive alligator. They have thousands of pressure sensors on their faces. The spots allow these tough reptiles to feel the ripples caused by even a single drop of water, and the alligator goes chomp, chomp, chomp!

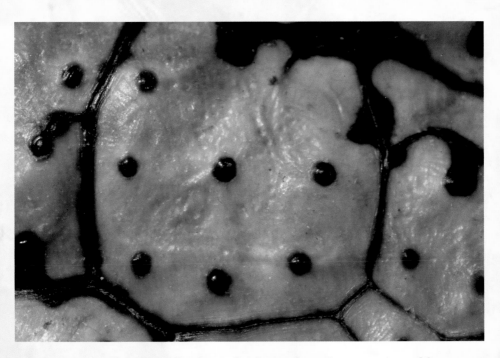

A close-up of the spots on the face of a saltwater crocodile, showing a detail of the pressure sensors.

3

SECRET OF THE PUKING PENGUINS REVEALED!

King penguins do not make nests. They incubate their only egg on top of their feet and cover it with their thick coat of feathers to keep it warm all the time until it hatches. King penguin parents take turns incubating the egg during the fifty-four days it takes for it to hatch. One parent keeps the egg at a steady temperature of 38°C (100.4°F), while the other parent takes a break to eat. The father usually has the last shift. While incubating the egg, dad penguins fast—do not eat at all—for about three weeks.[1]

No Fast Food for Penguins

Chick penguins have to eat soon after birth or they will die. Like many other birds, baby penguins eat regurgitated (thrown up) food from their

Close-up of a king penguin's head. Notice the typical colors of the feathers in the head and the long, sharp beak.

parents. If all goes well, mom penguin will be back by the time the baby hatches, and she will regurgitate the very important first meal to keep the chick alive. But what happens if mom is late returning from her feeding trip? Actually, scientists have estimated that by hatching time, four out of ten mother penguins are not back yet to feed the baby.[2]

Feeding is neither easy nor fast for king penguins. They have to swim the seas to feed. King penguins' favorite food seems to be lantern fish, which swim in large schools between the cold subantarctic waters and the colder Antarctic waters. Depending on how sea currents move, the fish may be moving closer or farther away from where the penguins live.[3]

Sometimes king penguins have to travel five hundred kilometers (about three hundred ten miles) from their colony looking for a meal that can be very hard to find. Mom penguins will keep looking for lantern fish until they find it; their babies' lives depend on it. But if moms take longer than expected to return, how will the on-duty dads keep the babies alive until the moms get home?

Not a Stomach Any More

Yvon Le Maho and his colleagues from Strasbourg, France, were intrigued by the king penguin's secret. The scientists traveled all the way to the Crozet Archipelago, a group of islands south of Madagascar, where a large colony of king penguins lives.

In the Crozet Islands, Le Maho and his colleagues observed that dad penguins regurgitated something to feed the baby chick when mom was late. But dad had not eaten for three weeks. His stomach should be empty by then.

The scientists decided to study the stomach contents of dad penguins to find out what the baby was eating. Michel Gauthier-Clerc, one of Le Maho's colleagues, carefully captured several penguins. Holding the penguin gently but firmly (penguins can peck), he slowly introduced a rubber tube in the penguin's beak until it reached the stomach. Then,

> **Meet the Scientists:**
> *Yvon Le Maho and his colleagues Michel Gauthier-Clerc and Cécile Thouzeau are physiologists (scientists who study how the body works). They are interested in understanding how animals, especially birds, adapt to the limits set by their natural environments.*

King penguin parents incubate their only egg on top of their feet and cover it with a flap of feathers to keep it warm. The bump at their feet is evidence of a hidden egg.

Gauthier-Clerc aspirated (sucked out) a small amount of the stomach contents and froze it in special containers. The scientist removed the tube and released the penguin. The penguins were not harmed by this and went back to what they were doing after the scientist released them.[4]

Back in their lab in France, Gauthier-Clerc analyzed what was inside the stomach. He was surprised! The father penguins had preserved food in their stomachs! There were pieces of whole fish, and they looked pretty much the same as freshly eaten food. Even though dad penguins had nothing else to eat, their stomachs had not digested the food to

SPECIAL STOMACH

The stomachs of egg-sitting penguins have other differences with the stomachs of non-incubating penguins that help them preserve the food:

The stomachs of egg-sitting penguins produce much less acid than the stomachs of penguins that are not incubating an egg. Acid helps digestion, or breaking the food down. Less acid means that the food is not as easily broken down or digested in the stomach.[5]

The stomachs of egg-sitting penguins "move" less than the stomachs of penguins not incubating an egg. Stomach motility (movement) helps digest the food too. By moving less, the stomach helps preserve food. [6]

nourish dad. Their stomachs did not work like stomachs anymore; they had become storage containers preserving food for the baby chick's survival.[7]

Science Tongue Twister:
Scientists call king penguins Aptenodytes patagonicus.

The scientists calculated that a father penguin's preserves were enough to feed a newborn chick for ten days. In this way mom had extra time to come back with more food. What prevented the food in dad penguin's stomach from being digested or even spoiled in three weeks?

No Microbes Allowed

Back in the Crozet Archipelago, the scientists captured more penguins and took stomach contents samples as before. Once they collected enough of these and froze them, they traveled back to their lab in France to find out the secret of the penguins' preserves.

Cécile Thouzeau, one of Le Maho's colleagues, studied the preserves. She discovered that they contained numerous bacteria. Bacteria are capable of spoiling food. Some of them cause diseases that might make the chick or the dad sick.

However, the bacteria in the preserves did not look healthy. They were alive, but looked deformed and damaged, so they could not spoil the food. Something in the stomach preserve was bad for the bacteria.[8]

Well-fed chicks grow fast and replace their fluffy baby feathers by molting.

Thouzeau studied what was inside the preserves and discovered numerous antimicrobial (microbe-fighting) substances. One of the antimicrobials was new; it had not been found anywhere before. Thouzeau called it "spheniscin" after the family name of the penguins, Spheniscidae. The amount of spheniscin in the stomachs of incubating penguins was much higher than in the stomachs of non-incubating birds.[9]

Thouzeau and her colleagues think that spheniscin and the other antimicrobials stop microbes from growing and spoiling the food in the penguin's stomach. In this way, if the chick hatches before mom penguin is back from the sea, it still has a healthy meal ready to eat.

> **King Penguin Fact:**
> *While fasting, egg-sitting dad penguins live off their body fat. They lose 20 percent of their weight every day.*[10]

4
A MASTER OF DISGUISE

ick Davies and Rebecca Kilner did not expect to hear a loud rattling sound at all. Actually, the noise had interrupted their sound-recording session; they would have to do it all over again. The rattle had come from a wooden box right beside them. The box contained a cuckoo bird chick in a nest. The scientists had set up their equipment to record the calls of the cuckoo chick begging for food. Davies tells the story:

> We were concerned to ensure the chick didn't get too cold, so we placed a small thermometer in the nest to record its temperature. The first time we did this, our recordings were interrupted by a loud clattering sound from inside the test box. The thermometer had apparently fallen

out of the nest. So we put it back. A few minutes later—the same clattering, and the thermometer, once again, was at the bottom of the box. Next time we watched—the cuckoo chick quickly balanced the thermometer on its back and heaved it out of the nest. It only settled down once it was sure it was the only occupant of the nest! After that, we gave up with the thermometer.[1]

Cuckoo bird chicks behave in ways not seen in other birds. It all begins every spring after the cuckoo mother lays her egg.

A Different Beginning

Cuckoo birds are different from other birds in that they do not build their own nests; they lay their eggs in other birds' nests. In east England, cuckoo moms seem to prefer reed warbler nests.

After the cuckoo mom lays her eggs—only one egg per nest—she leaves. She never comes back to check on her eggs or on her soon-to-hatch chicks.[2] How is a newly hatched cuckoo going to survive in a stranger's nest?

Cuckoo Chicks Go to Extremes to Survive

The warbler parents accept the cuckoo egg in their nest and incubate it together with their own eggs. They have accepted

A warbler's nest with three warbler eggs and one larger cuckoo egg. Notice that the cuckoo egg has a color and spotted pattern very similar to the warbler eggs; it is just a little bigger.

it because the cuckoo egg looks very much like warbler eggs. The cuckoo egg may be a bit bigger, but it is green and spotted like warbler eggs.[3]

The cuckoo chick hatches before the warbler chicks do. And from this time the cuckoo displays very unusual behavior. Only a few hours old, the featherless chick balances a warbler egg in a natural hollow in its back and at the same time it braces its legs against the sides of the nest. While holding its head down, the chick slowly pushes the egg to the rim of the nest. For its final move, the chick jerks the egg over the top of the nest. The chick falls to the bottom of the nest, exhausted.[4] This is a humongous job! The three-gram chick is working against a one-gram egg. It would be like a sixty-kilogram (about one hundred thirty pounds) person trying to push a

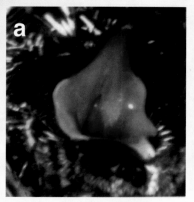
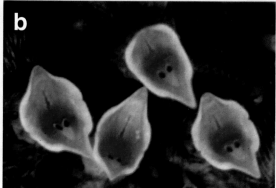

Compare the gape of a cuckoo chick (a) to gapes of four warbler chicks (b). Notice that the cuckoo chick has a gape that is bigger and of a different color than the warblers' gapes.

pack of forty water bottles (five hundred milliliters each) over the rim of a deep hole!

There are usually two more eggs to evict before the cuckoo has succeeded in reaching its goal: becoming the only chick warbler parents have to feed.

Uncovering the Secret of the Cuckoo's Deception

Amazingly, warbler parents do not take any action against the cuckoo that has destroyed their own eggs. Even then, warblers feed the larger cuckoo chick until it is ready to take care of itself. They feed it as often as they would feed four warbler chicks. With this amount of food, cuckoo chicks grow quickly to adult size. They grow to eight times the adult warbler's weight, overflowing and squashing the nest![5]

Davies and Kilner were puzzled. How can one cuckoo chick that is bigger and does not look like warbler chicks, trick warblers into feeding him for as long as thirty-three days?

Is Being Bigger Enough to Trick Warblers?

A five-to-eight-day-old cuckoo chick weighs about twenty-six grams, while a warbler chick of approximately the same age weighs just about eight grams. The scientists thought that maybe the cuckoo chick took advantage of its larger size. Maybe when warblers saw a large cuckoo chick in the nest, it was like seeing four of their own smaller chicks. Then warblers responded to this visual clue by bringing enough food for four warbler chicks to one cuckoo chick.

Davies and Kilner reasoned that if the cuckoo chick's larger size was sufficient to make warbler parents bring food for four to the nest, then similarly sized chicks of other types of birds should also receive food for four.[6]

They tested this idea by temporarily replacing warbler chicks in a nest with one blackbird chick or one song thrush chick. At seven days old, these chicks weigh about the same as one cuckoo chick of the same age. Then, the scientists observed while the chicks begged for food and the warbler parents fed them.

> **Meet the Scientists:**
> *Nick Davies and Rebecca Kilner are zoologists. They study animals, specifically how they modify their behavior to adapt to the changing conditions of their environment.*

A warbler parent observes chicks begging for food. The speaker to the right of the nest plays back chick calls during the experiments.

The warbler parents brought food to the blackbird and thrush chicks. However, they brought food less often for those than they did for one cuckoo chick of the same size. Actually, the warblers brought food to blackbirds and thrushes with the same frequency they brought food to one warbler chick, which was about one third of the weight of the blackbirds and thrushes.[7]

The experiment showed clear results. Having a larger size alone was not sufficient for a cuckoo chick to make its foster parents bring more food. But the parents do bring more food, so what trick do cuckoos have under their feathers?

Sing Like a Choir

If a cuckoo cannot trick warblers with its larger size alone, then, is the cuckoo deceiving its foster parents using its begging calls (sound clues)?

Like many other things about the cuckoo, the chicks' begging calls are very unusual. They call with a continuous and rapid "si, si, si." This call is very different from the begging call of a single warbler chick, which is much slower and sounds like "tsip . . . tsip . . . tsip." However, one cuckoo chick's begging call sounds amazingly similar to a whole brood or group of warbler chicks.[8] Is this imitation tricking the warblers?

Cuckoo Playbacks

Davies and Kilner thought that the cuckoo's trick was to imitate the calls of four warbler chicks begging together. If this was true, then when they played a recording of the cuckoo calls

beside a nest with one blackbird or thrush chick, the warbler parents should feed the single chick as often as they fed a cuckoo chick.

A cuckoo chick has grown and it almost does not fit in the nest. The warbler parent keeps feeding a chick that is bigger than she is!

To test this idea, they removed warbler chicks from a nest in the wild. They replaced them with one blackbird or one thrush chick that looked to be the same size as a cuckoo but sounded like a warbler. Then, the scientists attached a speaker right beside the nest and broadcast the recordings of cuckoo chick begging calls.

The scientists were amazed! When they played the cuckoo chick's recording, the warbler fed the blackbird chick as often as it would feed a cuckoo chick! But when the blackbird was left alone begging for food (no playback added), the warbler fed it as often as it would feed one warbler chick.[9]

Davies and Kilner had uncovered the secret of the cuckoo bird chick. This amazing bird is a master of disguise. The cuckoo chick begging calls imitate the calls of four warbler chicks. The warblers believe what their ears tell them and feed the cuckoo as often as they would feed a brood of four warblers. The cuckoo's amazing imitation of chick warbler's begging calls is its ticket to survival.

5
CATCHING
THE RAINBOW

Jian Zi was disappointed. It seemed that he had been cheated when he bought a handful of peacock feathers. He thought they were the real thing, but now a man had told him that the feathers were probably fake.[1]

Zi had bought the feathers because he was intrigued by their magnificent colors, especially in the "eye" design. He said, "When I saw the pattern against the sunshine, I was amazed by the stunning beauty of the feathers."[2] The colors are bright and shiny; they are "iridescent." This means that the colors change slightly depending on from which direction you look at the feather.

You have seen iridescence many times when the sun shines on the surface of soap bubbles or on oil spilled on the ground. Iridescent means "showing the colors of the rainbow." The first part of the world, "irid," comes from Latin and means rainbow.

Zi had great expectations. He wanted to discover the secret of the iridescence; but if the feathers were a fake, then his expectations could not be fulfilled. What could he do?

Color My World

When you want to color a picture, you reach for your markers, crayons, or paint. They provide many different colors thanks to pigments, which are chemicals that absorb certain colors and reflect others. For example, blue crayons are blue because the pigment absorbs all the colors except blue, which is reflected so you perceive it with your eyes.

In nature, pigments color many things. Take, for example, the color of your skin and your hair. Their color comes from the pigment called melanin. The more melanin in your hair, the darker the color.

Compared to people's hair, for example, bird feathers display countless colors. Many reds, yellows, and oranges are produced by pigments, but most blues, violets, and iridescent whites are not.[3] Besides using pigments, nature has another way to color the world, and this other way has a lot to do with what light is and how it behaves.

Playing With Light

One of the major contributions of Sir Isaac Newton (a famous eighteenth-century British scientist) was showing that white light is made up of the colors of the rainbow. You can see this clearly when white light enters a prism and then exits separated in all its different colors.

Newton also had something to say about the iridescence of peacock feathers. In 1730, he wrote in his book *Optiks* that

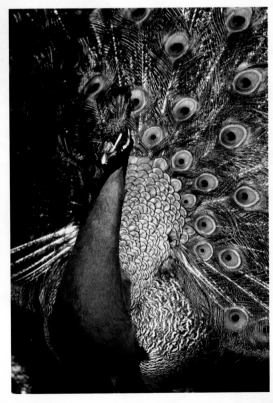

the iridescent colors were produced by the way the thin structure of the feathers interfered with light passing through them.[4]

Pigments do not give the peacock its astonishing colors. In this case, light passing

A male peacock showing a detail of the "eyes design" in its tail.

Detail of the "eye design" in the peacock's tail.

through the peacock's feathers separates into different colors. However, only some colors, not all the colors of the rainbow (like in the case of the prism), are seen after interacting with the feathers.

This means that besides pigments, nature colors the world by playing with light. Some animals have structures in their bodies, like bird feathers or the wings of butterflies, that are able to interfere with or change the way light moves when it goes through them. Bird feathers and butterfly wings separate the colors of the rainbow and reflect and refract the colors in different ways.

The result of "playing with light" is that some colors come up very shiny, others less shiny, and others disappear.

Playing with light creates an immense variety of color combinations. Just look at the peacock and other magnificent blue birds, as well as a diversity of butterflies, fish, beetles, and snakes. Wherever you see an animal with iridescent colors, you know it is playing with light.

It All Happens in the Nano-world

Scientists call "structural colors" those produced by "playing with light." They have that name because they are not caused by pigments but by the interaction of light with "structures" like those found in peacock feathers.

But what are those structures? How do they produce colors? To answer these questions, scientists looked at the structures of peacock feathers. Specifically, they looked at the smallest projections from the feather, called barbules. Using the naked eye, scientists could see that barbules that produce structural colors are very thin and flat, but they could not see many more details. So scientists looked closer.

Using a light microscope that makes objects look about one thousand times larger than their actual size, scientists saw something that looked like a pattern in the barbule structure. It seemed that structural colors are produced by micro-sized (very tiny) structures arranged in a certain pattern or order. But the barbule was still too small to tell exactly what the pattern was.[5]

Jian Zi and his colleagues had decided to look even closer at the barbules. If the feathers were fake, however, the scientists would not be able to learn anything from the research. After much thought, they decided to go ahead with their experiment.

They used an electron microscope. This instrument can magnify (make look larger) objects to fifty thousand times their actual size; some even more. Zi was fascinated by what he saw.

Like a Crystal

Zi and his colleagues looked at the structures of blue, green, and yellow barbules in the feathers that form the "eyes" in the peacock's tail.

The electron microscope showed Zi that the surface of the barbules was formed by many ultra thin layers running

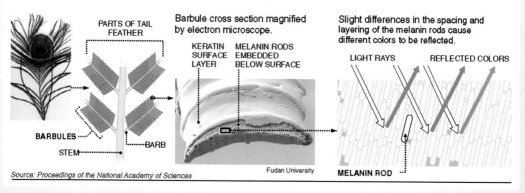

Color Without Pigment

Generally, color is caused by pigments. But scientists have discovered that the brilliant colors of the peacock's tail feathers are caused by microscopic reflective rods in the tiny barbules that line each of the feather's barbs.

PARTS OF TAIL FEATHER

BARBULES

STEM

BARB

Barbule cross section magnified by electron microscope.

KERATIN SURFACE LAYER

MELANIN RODS EMBEDDED BELOW SURFACE

Fudan University

Slight differences in the spacing and layering of the melanin rods cause different colors to be reflected.

LIGHT RAYS

REFLECTED COLORS

MELANIN ROD

Source: Proceedings of the National Academy of Sciences

parallel to the barbule's surface, like a stack of papers laying on the surface of a table. Each layer was made of numerous melanin rods of about the same size. The rods were connected with keratin (the same substance that forms your fingernails), which acted like a glue to keep the rods together, forming a thin layer. The rods within a layer were not set in a disordered fashion. They were laid one beside another in an ordered manner, almost like tiles on a kitchen floor.[6] This order, almost like a crystal, is what allows the barbules to play with light. The feathers were not fake after all!

Making Different Colors

All the barbules, regardless of their color, were formed by ordered layers of melanin rods. Zi wondered, if all the barbules have the same micro-structure, how can they make different colors? Using the electron microscope, Zi took some measurements. He measured the air-filled space between the layers of rods and the number of melanin rod layers in barbules of different colors.

The results were, in Zi's words, "very ingenious and rather simple." He found that blue barbules were made of nine to twelve layers of melanin rods, spaced about one hundred forty nanometers (nm) apart. Green barbules were made also of nine to twelve layers of melanin rods, but the spacing between layers was one hundred fifty nanometers. This nano-difference is enough for the barbule to play differently with

HOW SMALL IS A NANOMETER?

To imagine how small a nanometer is, pretend that you have a string one meter long (about 3.3 feet). Now, use your imagination and divide the string into one million equal parts. Each one of these sections is one millionth of a meter (a micrometer; "micro" means a millionth). Finally, divide one millionth of a meter into one thousand equal parts. Each one of them is a nanometer. One nanometer is too small for our naked eyes to see. The spacing between layers of melanin rods and the wavelength of different colors are both hundreds of nanometers long.

light and produce green instead of blue. Even at the nano-level size matters! Yellow barbules had about six layers of melanin rods spaced 165 nm apart.[7]

Zi and his colleagues had discovered the secret of the peacock's colors. Peacocks have succeeded at catching colors of the rainbow by developing barbules that have a highly-ordered structure at the microscopic level—almost like a crystal. The ordered nano-structure has a pattern of successive layers of melanin rods. By changing the number of layers and the spacing between them, the thin, flat surface of the barbules captures the shimmering hues displayed by the beautiful peacock.

★ CHAPTER NOTES ★

Chapter 1. What a Grip!

1. Personal interview with Dr. Anthony Herrel, April 17, 2007.
2. Anthony Herrel, et al., "The Mechanics of Prey Prehension in Chameleons," *The Journal of Experimental Biology*, vol. 203, no. 21, 2000, pp. 3255–3263.
3. Ibid., p. 3262.
4. Personal interview with Dr. Anthony Herrel, April 17, 2007.
5. Herrel, et al., p. 3261.
6. Anthony Herrel, et al., "Functional Implications of Supercontracting Muscle in the Chameleon Tongue Retractors," *The Journal of Experimental Biology*, vol. 204, 2001, pp. 3621–3627.
7. Personal interview with Dr. Anthony Herrel, April 17, 2007.
8. Herrel, et al., "The Mechanics of Prey Prehension in Chameleons," p. 3261.
9. Personal interview with Dr. Anthony Herrel, April 17, 2007.
10. Ibid.
11. Anthony Herrel, et al., "Morphology and Histochemistry of the Hyolingual Apparatus in Chameleons," *Journal of Morphology*, vol. 249, 2001, pp. 154–170.
12. Jurriaan de Groot and Johan van Leeuwen, "Evidence for an Elastic Projection Mechanism in the Chameleon Tongue," *Proceedings of the Royal Society London B*, vol. 271, no. 1540, April 7, 2004, p. 761.
13. Ulrike K. Müller and Sander Kranenbarg, "Power at the Tip of the Tongue," *Science*, vol. 304, no. 5668, April 9, 2004, pp. 217–218.

Chapter 2. Alligator Feelings

1. Personal interview with Dr. Daphne Soares, April 20, 2007.

2. Ibid.

3. Ibid.

4. Daphne Soares, "Neurology: An Ancient Sensory Organ in Crocodilians," *Nature*, vol. 417, no. 6886, 2002, pp. 241–242.

5. Ibid., p. 241.

6. Personal interview with Dr. Daphne Soares, April 20, 2007.

7. Soares, p. 241.

8. Ibid., p. 242.

Chapter 3. The Secret of the Puking Penguins Revealed!

1. Michel Gauthier-Clerc, et al., "Ecophysiology: Penguin Fathers Preserve Food for Their Chicks," *Nature*, vol. 408, no. 6815, December 21–28, 2000, pp. 928–929.

2. Ibid., p. 928.

3. "Something Special From the Subantarctic," *French Science and Technology*, no. 47, March 2004, p. 1.

4. Gauthier-Clerc, et al., p. 928.

5. Cécile Thouzeau, et al., "Adjustments of Gastric pH, Motility and Temperature During Long-term Preservation of Stomach Contents in Free-ranging Incubating King Penguins," *The Journal of Experimental Biology*, vol. 207, 2004, pp. 2715–2724.

6. Ibid.

7. Gauthier-Clerc, et al., p. 928.

8. Cécile Thouzeau, et al., "Evidence of Stress in Bacteria Associated With Long-term Preservation of Food in the Stomach of Incubating King Penguins (*Aptenodytes patagonicus*)," *Polar Biology*, vol. 26, 2003, pp. 115–123.

9. Cécile Thouzeau, et al., "Speniscins, Avian Beta-defensins in Preserved Stomach Contents of the King Penguin, *Aptenodytes patagonicus*," *The Journal of Biological Chemistry*, vol. 278, no. 51, 2003, pp. 51053–51058.

10. Gauthier-Clerc, et al., p. 928.

Chapter 4. Master of Disguise

1. Personal interview with Dr. Nick Davies, May 4, 2007.
2. Nick Davies, *Cuckoos, Cowbirds, and Other Cheats* (London: T&AD Poyser, 2000), p. 4.
3. Nick Davies, "Cuckoo Tricks With Eggs and Chicks," *British Birds*, March 2002, pp. 101–115.
4. Davies, *Cuckoos, Cowbirds, and Other Cheats*, p. 1.
5. Ibid.
6. Davies, "Cuckoo Tricks With Eggs and Chicks," p. 101.
7. Nick Davies, Rebecca Kilner, and David Noble, "Nestling Cuckoos, *Cuculus canorus*, Exploit Hosts With Begging Calls That Mimic a Brood," *Proceedings of the Royal Society London B*, vol. 265, 1998, pp. 676.
8. Ibid., p. 674.
9. Ibid., p. 675.

Chapter 5. Catching the Rainbow

1. Personal interview with Dr. Jian Zi, May 7, 2007.
2. Ibid.
3. Elizabeth Pennisi, "Shedding Light on Avian Iridescence," *Science*, vol. 299, no. 5606, January 24, 2003, p. 504.
4. Steven K. Blau, "Light as a Feather: Structural Elements Give Peacock Plumes Their Color," *Physics Today*, January 2004, p. 18.
5. Pete Vukusic and J. Roy Sambles, "Photonic Structures in Biology," *Nature*, vol. 424, August 14, 2003, pp. 852–855.
6. Jian Zi, et al., "Coloration Strategies in Peacock Feathers," *Proceedings of the National Academy of Sciences, USA*, vol. 100, no. 22, October 28, 2003, pp. 12576–12578.
7. Ibid., p. 12577.

★ GLOSSARY ★

barbule ★ A slender strand attached to the thicker middle body of a feather called the shaft.

brood ★ The young of an animal, usually birds, that are born and reared together.

electrode ★ A tool through which electricity enters or leaves.

infrared light ★ A type of radiation people cannot see with their eyes unless they use special goggles.

iridescence ★ Having rainbow colors that appear to move or change as the angle at which they are seen changes.

mucus ★ A clear, slimy substance.

nerve ★ A bundle of fibers that transmits messages between the brain and the body.

neuroscientist ★ A scientist that studies the nervous system.

prey ★ Animals that are caught, killed, and eaten by other animals as food.

prism ★ A transparent solid object with flat faces that looks like a pyramid and is used to separate white light into the colors of the rainbow.

sensor ★ A device capable of detecting and responding to stimuli such as movement, light, or heat.

stimuli ★ Something that causes a physical response in an organism (The singular form of the word is *stimulus*.)

★ FURTHER READING ★

Books

Johnson, Jinny. *Birds (1000 Things You Should Know)*. Great Bardfield, Essex, England: Miles Kelly Publishers, Ltd., 2005.

Lockwood, Sophie. *Chameleons (The World of Reptiles)*. Chanhassen, Minn.: Child's World, 2006.

Parker, Steve. *Penguins, Peacocks, and Other Birds*. Minneapolis, Minn.: Compass Point Books, 2005.

Simon, Seymour. *Crocodiles and Alligators*. New York: HarperTrophy, 2001.

Internet Addresses

Video of a Chameleon Feeding
http://www.greatestplaces.org/medias/video/chameleon.mov

Infrared Movies of Dr. Soares's Experiments with Alligators
http://www.wam.umd.edu/~daph/DPR.html

Cuckoo Bird Calls
http://www.rspb.org.uk/wildlife/birdguide/name/c/cuckoo/index.asp

Ana María Rodríguez's Homepage
http://www.anamariarodriguez.com

★ INDEX ★